The Benjamin Generation

Joseph Prince

All Scripture quotations, unless otherwise indicated, are taken from the New King James Version. Copyright © 1982 by Thomas Nelson, Inc. Used by permission. All rights reserved.

The Benjamin Generation

ISBN 981-05-2474-9
© Copyright Joseph Prince, 2006

Joseph Prince Teaching Resources
www.josephprince.com

Printed in the Republic of Singapore
First edition, fourteenth print: July 2012

contents

1

The End-Time Generation Of Grace

chapter 1

The End-Time Generation Of Grace

The Last Generation

We are living in prophetic times. In times like these, God is revealing prophetic truths that are going to be a great blessing for His church. You see, prophetic teaching has the ability to pass on what was spoken hundreds, even thousands, of years ago into the "here and now". What was spoken of back then becomes relevant for us today.

One key prophetic truth that I believe God wants to make known to us is that before Jesus comes again for His people, the last generation will become known as the Benjamin Generation. In fact, the Lord spoke to me and said, "The Benjamin Generation is here."

> What marks the Benjamin Generation is not God's judgment but His grace.

Now, I've heard about the Joshua Generation, but I've never heard of the Benjamin Generation. So when God said that, I immediately remembered that Benjamin was the last son of Jacob. I began to realise what the Lord was saying — that the Benjamin Generation will be the last generation before Jesus comes again!

A Generation Of Grace

When I received this revelation, I began to study the life of Benjamin and I found that the Benjamin Generation is a generation of grace. Today, God wants His people to know that the end-time church is the Benjamin Generation. And what marks this generation is not God's judgment, but His grace.

Grace is unmerited, unearned and undeserved favour. In these end times, God wants to emphasise to His people that His blessings come by grace alone.

You will find that Benjamin's life was a life of undeserved favour and blessing. When Joseph and Benjamin were reunited, the first words Joseph spoke to Benjamin were words of grace. When Joseph saw his youngest brother, he said, *"God be gracious to you, my son."* (Genesis 43:29)

Another important feature of Benjamin is that the number five is stamped all over his life. The number five speaks of God's abundant provision through His grace. Though all the brothers ate at Joseph's table, the Bible says that *"Benjamin's serving was five times as much"*. (Genesis 43:34) Later, in Genesis 45:22, we see reference to this number again — *"to Benjamin he [Joseph] gave… five changes of garments"*.

Whenever the number five appears in the Bible, you will see God's grace being manifested. The children of Israel offered five offerings.

(Leviticus 1–7) David brought five smooth stones with him when he went to face Goliath. (1 Samuel 17:40) And Jesus multiplied five loaves to feed 5,000 people. (Mark 6:37–44)

So we see that Benjamin symbolises God's grace. Likewise, the last generation before Jesus returns is a generation of grace. And if grace is God's unmerited, unearned favour, then we are the generation that will experience His undeserved favour, His grace.

Even the way in which Benjamin received his name shows us a picture of God's grace. When he was born, his mother Rachel named him Ben-Oni, which means "son of my sorrow". But his father Jacob intervened and changed his name to Benjamin, which means "son of my right hand". (Genesis 35:18) We know that the right hand is the hand of favour, the hand which brings His help. The psalmist declared, *"Your right hand upholds me."* (Psalm 63:8)

Isn't that beautiful? When we were born, our destiny was to be Ben-Onis, sons of sorrow. But because of what Jesus did on the cross, we are now Benjamins, sons of His right hand. Jesus took our place at the cross because Isaiah 53:3

tells us that He became a *"Man of sorrows"*. He did that so that we might become sons of His right hand, seated in the place of favour. Ephesians 2:6 declares that God *"raised us up together, and made us sit together in the heavenly places in Christ Jesus"*. This is what marks us, the end-time church, as the Benjamin Generation.

> Don't be quick to believe prophecies that strike fear in God's people.

Gloom In The World, Glory In The Church

Some people are surprised to hear that God is going to bless the end-time church through His unmerited favour. My friend, are you surprised? Some people are so conditioned to hearing doom-and-gloom preaching about the end times. They hear preachers tell them that in the end times, darkness will cover us all.

In fact, some years ago, I heard a "prophecy" that Singapore would fall into the hands of foreign powers and parts of Australia would literally slip under the sea. I stood against this "prophecy" because people were photocopying and distributing all this bad news and calling it "prophecy". Don't be quick to believe such "prophecies" which strike fear in God's people. God does not give prophecies to frighten His people.

Instead, the Apostle Paul said that *"he who prophesies speaks edification and exhortation and comfort to men"*. (1 Corinthians 14:3) Isn't it just like God to use prophecies to edify, exhort and comfort His people rather than put fear in them? As for those "prophecies", many years have come and gone, and none of them have come to pass.

If you are one of those who have been plagued by fear because of doom-and-gloom prophecies, I have good news, my friend. It is true that Isaiah 60:2 declares, *"For behold, the darkness shall cover the earth, and deep darkness the people..."* But it does not stop there. The second part of that verse says, *"But the Lord will arise over you, and His glory will be seen upon you."*

So although darkness will cover the people in the world, the Lord will arise over us, His people. He will pour His glory on us.

Protection And Provision For The Benjamin Generation

It's obvious that the world is getting darker and darker, but be encouraged that you are not of this world. You are a child of God. When the devil makes the world darker with terrorism, earthquakes, tsunamis, new strains of viruses and all kinds of evil things, the Word of God tells us to get ready because our light will be seen.

In other words, as the world gets darker, the church will be blessed more and more. The Bible says that the path of the righteous shines brighter and brighter until the perfect day when Christ returns. (Proverbs 4:18) And we are the righteousness of God in Christ Jesus, so our path is getting brighter and brighter!

We have nothing but increasing light to look forward to. As the Benjamin Generation, we have only good in front of us. And those who believe this will experience it... even in the midst of darkness.

I have a Sri Lankan student in my church whose father was born again during one of our services in June 2004. His mother dedicated her life to Christ shortly after that. They live in Colombo, the capital city of Sri Lanka, and their hometown is very close to the sea. When the tsunami crashed on their shores on 26 December 2004, they were spared because the entire family had gone to visit an aunt who lived further inland.

After the killer wave had subsided, the family members made their way home to see what damage the tsunami had left behind. They discovered that the tsunami had stopped just three houses from their home! God didn't just protect them, He also preserved all their possessions! Isn't God good? The devil wanted that family to be Ben-Onis — sons of sorrow — but Jesus intervened for His Benjamins — sons of His right hand of favour.

> The more your eyes are opened to see Jesus in His glory in the Old Testament, the more you will understand the New Testament.

We are the Benjamin Generation. Like the Sri Lankan family, we can expect to be protected, preserved and prospering in these last days... all because of His unmerited, unearned, undeserved favour!

How Can We Spiritualise The Life Of Benjamin?

Some of you might say, "Pastor Prince, all this sounds very nice, but what gives you the right to spiritualise the life of Benjamin and say that it is a picture of the end-time church?" Well, we must understand that the New (Testament) is in the Old concealed and the Old (Testament) is in the New revealed.

Let me explain. The Old Testament is filled with hidden pictures of Jesus as well as new covenant truths. The King of glory appears in the Old Testament as types, symbols and shadows. And the more your eyes are opened to see Jesus in His glory in the Old Testament, the more you will understand the New Testament.

Paul Used Old Testament Types And Shadows To Teach New Testament Truths

Let me explain further by showing you how the Apostle Paul used Old Testament types to teach New Testament truths.

Galatians 4:21–31

[21]Tell me, you who desire to be under the law, do you not hear the law? [22]For it is written that Abraham had two sons: the one by a bondwoman, the other by a freewoman. [23]But he who was of the bondwoman was born according to the flesh, and he of the freewoman through promise, [24]which things are symbolic. For these are the two covenants: the one from Mount Sinai which gives birth to bondage, which is Hagar — [25]for this Hagar is Mount Sinai in Arabia, and corresponds to Jerusalem which now is, and is in bondage with her children — [26]but the Jerusalem above is free, which is the mother of us all. [27]For it is written: "Rejoice, O barren, you who do not bear! Break forth and

shout, you who are not in labour! For the desolate has many more children than she who has a husband." 28Now we, brethren, as Isaac was, are children of promise. 29But, as he who was born according to the flesh then persecuted him who was born according to the Spirit, even so it is now. 30Nevertheless what does the Scripture say? "Cast out the bondwoman and her son, for the son of the bondwoman shall not be heir with the son of the freewoman." 31So then, brethren, we are not children of the bondwoman but of the free.

Here, Paul said that these two women symbolise two mountains, which represent the two covenants. Hagar represents the old covenant, which is the law or the Ten Commandments. And Sarah represents the new covenant, which is grace.

Now, the law is from Mount Sinai. And what does Paul say that the law or the Ten Commandments produces? Freedom? No, he says that the law produces bondage! On the other hand, grace is from the heavenly Jerusalem and grace brings freedom.

It was not Abraham but Sarah who could not produce children. And both of them tried to help God keep His promise to them that they would bear a son. When Sarah gave her bondmaid Hagar to Abraham, Ishmael was born. Hagar, who represents the law, produced Ishmael who *"was born according to the flesh"*. (Galatians 4:23)

> If you want to inherit the promises of God, don't trust in your human performance. Instead, look to His promises.

Can you see from this passage what the flesh represents? The flesh represents self-effort or human strength. Ishmael was born according to the flesh. In other words, he was born out of human effort. Now, note what Paul said about human effort — *"… those who are in the flesh cannot please God."* (Romans 8:8) What Paul means is that God is not pleased when we trust in our human strength.

Sarah, on the other hand, gave birth to Isaac, not through the flesh, not through human effort, but through the Spirit. By that time, Abraham was very old and his body was as good as dead. And Sarah, who was barren, had become doubly barren. No amount of human effort could have produced a child for Abraham and Sarah. It was in that moment when no amount of self-effort or human strength could achieve results that Isaac was born. He was born through the Spirit, through God's promise. It pleases God when we trust in His promises.

If you want to inherit the promises of God, don't play around with the law, don't trust in your human performance. Instead, look to His promises. Under grace, the barren can rejoice for the desolate will have many more children than she who has a husband. (Galatians 4:27)

That's why Paul concluded in Galatians 4:30 that we are to cast out the bondwoman. What does he mean? He is telling us to remove the law. Don't play around with the law. Don't listen to people who preach the law. The law brings death. When the law was first given, 3,000 people died. (Exodus 32:28) But the Spirit gives life. When

God poured out His Spirit on Pentecost, 3,000 people were born again! (Acts 2:41)

By showing us how Sarah and Hagar represent the two covenants, Paul set a precedent for the use of types and symbols. In the same way, God is painting a picture of Benjamin as a symbol or type of the end-time church. And I believe He did it because He wants us to know that before Jesus comes again, He will raise up a generation of grace, a generation who knows His unmerited favour. And all that is possible because Jesus became the Son of sorrow so that we can be sons of God's right hand, sons of His favour.

chapter

2

Why Grace?

chapter 2
Why Grace?

God Wants Us Blessed

We now know that the Benjamin Generation is the end-time generation. And we have also established that Benjamin typifies grace. But why does God want a generation of grace in these end times?

I believe it is because God found fault with the first covenant of law. That's the reason why Jesus came to establish a new covenant of grace. Paul said, *"For if that first covenant had been faultless, then no place would have been sought for a second. Because finding fault with them, He says: 'Behold, the days are coming, says the Lord, when I will make a new covenant with the house of Israel and with the house of Judah — not according to the covenant that I made with their fathers...*" (Hebrews 8:7–9)

Aren't you glad that God found fault with the old covenant? Under the old covenant, you are blessed only if you obey. And if you fail to obey just one law, you are guilty of breaking all the laws! James said it this way, *"For whoever shall keep the whole law, and yet stumble in one point, he is guilty of all."* (James 2:10)

God found fault with that because you and I know that under such a covenant, it is not possible for anyone to be blessed. Paul also made it clear that the old law was not functioning — *"He has made the first obsolete. Now what is becoming obsolete and growing old is ready to vanish away."* (Hebrews 8:13)

Thankfully, because the old covenant is now obsolete, God does not apply it to us today.

It is old and outdated! So if you are still striving to abide by the old covenant, you are missing out on God's blessing because God has given us a new covenant. In these end times, if you insist on holding on to the old covenant, you are missing out on God's blessing.

God says that the new covenant will not be like the old. In what way is it not like the old? Well, under the old covenant, if you obey the laws, you are blessed. And you must obey all the laws to be blessed. Some people try to explain the old covenant to me this way, "Pastor Prince, God just wants us to try our best to keep whatever law we can." My friend, if you believe that, then you don't understand the holiness of God.

If you want to be under the old covenant or the covenant of law, then you have to obey **all** the laws. You cannot pick and choose. You cannot say, "This law is not a problem for me, it's easy, I can obey it. But this one over here is quite difficult, I think God will understand if I don't obey it."

In Leviticus 19:37, God said, *"Therefore you shall observe **all** My statutes and **all** My judgments, and perform them: I am the Lord."* When God says

all, He means **all**! You cannot pick and choose which laws to obey.

Now, do you understand why God found fault with the old covenant? There is no way we can be blessed if we are under this covenant. That is why Jesus brought in the new covenant. And by the way, you cannot mix the two covenants. You have to choose between the two. You are either under one or the other.

This new covenant is not like the old covenant. Under the old covenant, you are blessed only if you obey. But under the new covenant, you and I are blessed because of Jesus' obedience at the cross. And He obeyed perfectly. That is why God can pour the fullness of His blessings on us.

> If you try to fulfil the law to be blessed, you will become tired because you have to depend on your own efforts.

Aren't you glad that He has established the new covenant? Isn't God good? He wants a generation of grace because it is only through the covenant of grace that He can pour His blessings on us, the Benjamin end-time generation.

Grace Brings Blessings, The Law Blinds

The life of Benjamin's mother Rachel is a picture of how we the Benjamin Generation will experience God's blessings through His undeserved favour. Rachel symbolises the covenant of grace. Leah, who is Rachel's sister and Benjamin's step-mother, symbolises the covenant of law.

Leah or *Le'ah* in Hebrew, means "weary". In other words, the law makes you weary. If you try to obtain your blessings through the law, you will never make it. If you try to fulfil the law to be blessed, you will become tired because you have to depend on your own efforts.

On the other hand, Rachel means "ewe" or "female sheep". Her name is a picture of grace. It is a picture of how we are favoured by God today because Jesus, the sacrificial Lamb of God, took our place on the cross. On that cross, Jesus exhausted the full wrath of God for us. He took our beating so that we can receive His blessings.

Today, we can expect God's blessings not because of what we have or have not done, but because of what **He** has done. That, my friend, is grace.

Now, the opposite is true when you put yourself under the law. Look at the life of Jacob. He had two women in his life — Rachel and Leah. He loved Rachel, but he was tricked by his father-in-law Laban into marrying Leah.

> Stop trying to obey the law to be blessed.

How did that happen? How did he marry the wrong woman? It was because Jacob did not unveil the bride! He was in a hurry! The next morning, when he woke up beside Leah, he would have screamed, "Aaaah!" Leah with make-up on was not very pretty, but Leah first thing in the morning without make-up was much worse! No wonder today, it is a tradition for the minister to say, "You may now unveil the bride!" It ensures that the groom marries the right girl, right?

But there is a deeper meaning here. What does the veil represent? The veil is a picture of the law. The Bible declares in 2 Corinthians 3:14,

"But their minds were blinded. For until this day the same veil remains unlifted in the reading of the Old Testament, because the veil is taken away in Christ."

Can you see how Jacob was robbed of the love of his life by Laban? Jacob did not unveil the bride, so he was blinded. This tells us that the law blinds us. It causes us to be dispossessed. It causes us to be robbed of God's blessing. What's the solution? Remove the veil! Stop looking to the law to be justified. Stop trying to obey the law to be blessed.

God Loves Grace

Rachel's life also teaches us something else — it is a picture of how God loves grace, not law. You see, Leah was born first, so Rachel came after Leah. In the same way, grace came after the law.

Now, just because Jacob married two women, please don't say that I approve of men having two wives! Let me tell you that when you have two women in your life, you are in trouble!

Please, don't have two wives. In the past, God allowed this. But in this case, God is pointing to these two women as representing two different things — law and grace.

Some of you may ask, "Does God love the law or grace?" Well, if you want the answer, just look at the lives of these two women. Jacob loved Rachel, not Leah. Likewise, God loves grace, not the law. Remember that the Bible says that Leah was not pretty, but it says that Rachel was. Rachel was beautiful. Now, don't get me wrong. God is not saying that He dislikes ugly people. Not at all! He is simply showing us that the glory of grace surpasses that of the law. (2 Corinthians 3:7–11)

I know that the law is holy, but I also know that grace is beautiful. God does not love the law, He loves grace. And although He has to execute justice, although He has to enforce the law, above all, what God loves is grace and mercy. That is why He did away with the covenant of law and sent His Son to take our punishment. He did that so that we can experience His grace, His undeserved favour.

God Specialises In Miraculous Turnarounds

God's grace applies to our lives today. If you need God to intervene in your life right now, He can do it! Look what He did to Benjamin. In Genesis 45, we see that by His grace, God turned around every negative circumstance in the lives of Benjamin and his family. That's how He can also bring about supernatural turnarounds in our lives today. If you are experiencing disease or debt, if you have a rebellious son or a wayward daughter, whatever your situation, don't be anxious about it. God specialises in miraculous turnarounds.

Joseph's brothers threw him into a pit and he later landed in prison for a crime he didn't commit. If anyone had a good reason to be anxious, it was Joseph. But God turned all these events around in his favour. Joseph went to the pit and then to prison, but God's grace placed him in the palace!

After Joseph's brothers had sold him into slavery, they began to regret what they had done. They began to feel guilty. During the famine, they went to Egypt to get food. There, they came face-to-face with their long-lost brother, Joseph.

But they did not recognise him. After all, it had been 20 years!

Joseph later told them that he wanted Simeon to remain with him while the rest of the brothers returned home to get Benjamin. When this happened, Joseph's brothers thought their sin had finally found them out. They were at a loss because they knew that this would cause great anguish to their father. But by God's grace, He prospered even their mistake.

Don't get me wrong. I am not saying that it is all right to be jealous of your brothers and to sell them out. No, what I am saying is that God can override the evil of man, and introduce His own purpose and plan into any situation. Though Joseph's brothers meant evil against him, God turned it around for good. (Genesis 50:20) By selling Joseph into slavery, they were actually giving him a free trip to the land where he would later save them all from famine.

Now, please don't follow Joseph's story to the letter. Please don't go out and say, "Well, I'm going to do something bad to someone so that God can turn it around for good." That is not how God works. In fact, when we fall into sin, when we make mistakes, it can hurt people. But God by His grace can override even all these. Isn't that beautiful? He really puts the amazing back into grace!

Listen to Joseph's words to his brothers. His words were like music to their ears:

Genesis 45:5,7–8
[5]But now, do not therefore be grieved or angry with yourselves because you sold me here; for God sent me before you to preserve life... [7]And God sent me before you to preserve a posterity for you in the earth, and to save your lives by a great deliverance. [8]So now it was not you who sent me here, but God; and He has made me a father to Pharaoh, and lord of all his house, and a ruler throughout all the land of Egypt.

As for Jacob, when he was told that Benjamin had been summoned to Egypt, he was beside himself. He did not want to give up Benjamin whom he had fathered with Rachel. Remember Rachel was the wife whom he loved. With Joseph and Simeon gone, there was no way he would give up this son. He cried out, *"All these things are against me."* (Genesis 42:36) Little did he know that Joseph, his beloved son, was actually planning all this for him. Though he did not know it, God was working behind the scenes for his good.

When you are in the midst of a recession, all you see are financial obstacles. But God sees your problem as a divine opportunity for good. God may see your problem as a divine opportunity for promotion, salary increase or new business clients.

> He delights in loving-kindness. He loves to show grace to His people.

Jacob thought that everything was working against him. That's the way he saw it. But in actual fact, the end result was that Pharaoh reserved the best of the land for him! God had everything planned for Jacob. And everything worked together for his good.

My friend, God's favour and grace will deliver the same for you. Know that if you put God first and trust in Him, whatever you are going through will work out in your favour. Your life is not an accident. You may have been born out of wedlock, but God loves you and He has a special plan for you.

Joseph's life was amazing. He went from the pit to the palace! God really turned everything around for Joseph. It was an extreme change in circumstances. Pharaoh trusted him so much that he put everything under Joseph's charge and gave him the name Zaphnath-Paaneah (Genesis 41:45), which means "saviour of the world". So Joseph literally went from being slave to saviour of the world. God promoted him so that he could preserve a posterity for His people.

What God did for Joseph, He can do for us. What God did for Benjamin and his family, He can also do for us, the Benjamin Generation. And all this will happen not because we deserve it, but because He delights in lovingkindness. He loves to show grace to His people.

A 180-Degree Change

I have many people in my church whose lives will testify to how God's grace brings radical turnarounds. We have a brother in our church who was once a hopeless drunk. He was on the verge of divorce when he came to our church and received Christ as his Saviour. His marriage had broken down beyond repair. Because he was a manager in the food and beverage industry, drinking was an occupational requirement that went from being a hazard to an addiction. He also smoked like a chimney, puffing up to 40 cigarettes a day.

After becoming a Christian in 1999, he tried to break free from the bottle, but he found that he couldn't. This brother had begun drinking when he was 15 and so he felt it would be impossible to quit.

One day, he heard me share a testimony of how another brother, who had been bound to the same addiction, had experienced total deliverance from alcohol. For the first time, he began to entertain the possibility of becoming dry, of breaking the addiction.

He decided that he would do what the other brother had done. So he picked up some of my audio tapes with the messages he wanted to hear. Every Friday night, he would listen to my tapes, especially the one where I shared the other brother's testimony. Because he was still bound to the bottle, he would buy six cans of beer and down them one by one as he listened to my tapes. As he listened and drank, he would confess the portion of scripture which brought the other brother deliverance from alcohol addiction. He would declare, "I am the righteousness of God in Christ!" (2 Corinthians 5:21)

I find this brother's testimony really interesting because another characteristic that will mark the Benjamin Generation is the righteousness of God. Why? Remember that Benjamin means "son of my right hand"? Well, Isaiah 41:10 says, *"Fear not, for I am with you; be not dismayed, for I am your God. I will strengthen you, yes, I will help you, I will uphold you with My righteous right hand."*

Notice that the right hand symbolises God's righteousness. So the Benjamin Generation, the sons of the right hand, will be marked by His righteousness.

But don't confuse righteousness with right behaviour. Righteousness is a gift. Paul said that *"those who receive abundance of grace and of the **gift** of righteousness will reign in life through the One, Jesus Christ".* (Romans 5:17)

Like David, this brother understood *"the blessedness of the man to whom God imputes righteousness **apart** from works"*. (Romans 4:6) He knew that he could not do anything to achieve righteousness. It is a gift that Jesus died for him to receive.

Every Friday night, that brother just kept believing that he had been made righteous because of what Jesus did on the cross, not because of anything he had or had not done. He kept seeing himself righteous in Christ. He kept believing that he had been justified (which means made righteous) by faith and not works. He kept believing that he was righteous and that he could not lose this righteousness, even though he was still drinking.

This continued for about eight to nine months. Despite repeatedly downing cans of beer, those nights of listening to the Word and confessing his righteousness strangely caused his desire for alcohol and cigarettes to grow weaker and weaker. At the same time, his love for Jesus grew stronger and stronger.

The consciousness of his righteousness became so overwhelming that he smoked his last cigarette and drank his last drop of alcohol at the end of 2000. Since then, he has not drunk a drop or smoked another cigarette.

Around that time, he sensed God telling him to leave the food and beverage industry, so he quit without having another job lined up. Within months, he was offered another job. His salary is now more than double the salary he received as a manager in the food and beverage industry.

In 2002, he met and fell in love with a beautiful sister in the church and they tied the knot in 2004. Today, he serves in the church choir and you would never guess his past addictions! God's grace and goodness, and this brother's revelation of how righteous he is in Christ, have brought about a 180-degree change in his life. He is now more prosperous financially, no longer addicted to alcohol and cigarettes, married, and his current job allows him so much more free time for his family!

Grace Produces True Holiness

Can you now see why God loves grace and not the law? The law can only produce outward and temporal change, but grace produces inward and permanent change. Grace produces true holiness. Only the grace of God has the power to make a drunk desire Jesus more than the bottle.

Grace not only makes you avoid sin, it will make you fall in love with Jesus and with His righteousness. Do you know why some men don't commit adultery? It is not because they love holiness. Some just don't have the money to do it. Some don't have the opportunity to do it. Some are afraid their wives will find out. Some fear punishment because there are strict laws in some countries against adultery. But these are not good reasons for not committing adultery.

> God's grace will make you love your wife so much that you won't want to commit adultery.

God wants us to stay faithful to our wives because we love them. You can actually keep the law — "Thou shall not commit adultery" — and still not love your wife. But the way you stay in love with your wife, the way you live a holy life, is to have grace in your life. Only God's grace can produce true holiness. God's grace will make you love your wife so much that you won't want to commit adultery.

Grace May Not Produce Immediate Results

Sometimes, grace does not produce immediate results. Just look at Rachel, a picture of grace. She bore her first son Joseph only after Leah and the bondmaids had given Jacob 10 sons!

To some people, the law appears to be very attractive. For instance, the law can seem very productive. It produced 10 sons for Leah and the bondmaids. The law seems to bring about immediate results. That's why some people don't like to talk about grace. They want things to happen **now**. They aren't prepared to wait for grace to work in their lives. But you must understand that instant change is seldom lasting change.

People who want immediate results resort to self-effort, to using the flesh. Rachel wanted to bear children just like Leah who had four boys —

Reuben, Simeon, Levi and Judah. So Rachel gave her bondmaid Bilhah to Jacob. And guess what, ladies? Jacob didn't seem to complain! So Bilhah bore two sons for Jacob — Dan and Naphtali. Rachel was impatient. Since God didn't seem to be doing anything, she felt that she needed to help God. Friends, this is not God's way.

Some church leaders are like that. They will tell young converts to do this and that, to behave this way and that way, to give up this and that. They want to see instant changes in these babes in Christ.

Don't get me wrong. I am not saying that we should allow new believers to continue in their old sinful ways. What I am saying is why not allow these new converts to first grow in the love of God, to first experience His grace? Paul said, *"For sin shall not have dominion over you, for you are not under law but under grace."* (Romans 6:14)

When we allow people to experience grace, sin will not have dominion over them. Those evil habits will fall away as a result of God's grace in their lives. Now, I didn't say that. The Apostle Paul did. He also said that it is the goodness of God that leads us to repentance. (Romans 2:4)

When we are patient with new believers, when we let them experience God's goodness, true and lasting change will come. When we let them know that God does not condemn them, I believe that they will have the strength to *"go and sin no more"*. Isn't that what Jesus told the woman who was caught in adultery? (John 8:11)

Grace Is Free But It Is Not Cheap — It Cost God His Son!

When we preach grace this way, when we say that today, God deals with His people based on undeserved favour, based on grace, some people call this "sloppy agape". You see, some people mistakenly think grace is a licence to sin. That's why some people think this is "crazy grace".

Such people will ask me, "So Pastor Prince, does that mean that I can go and kill someone now, and God will still be gracious to me?" These people seem to get the idea that grace means God has gone soft on sin.

My friend, grace does not mean that God has gone soft on sin. He is not looking down from heaven, shaking his head and saying, "Boys will be boys!" He is not saying, "Never mind, it's okay to sin a little." As a righteous God, He hates sin and He has to punish sin, every single sin. In fact, He **has** punished your sins and my sins, and He has done this in the body of His Son. Today, you and I are forgiven because another was punished.

Grace may be free for you, but it cost God everything. It cost God His Son.

That is why Paul said in Hebrews 10:17 that our sins and our lawless deeds He remembers no more. This is because at the cross, God remembered all our sins in the body of His Son. So today, He no longer counts our sins against us. (2 Corinthians 5:18–19) This, my friends, is grace.

Paul describes it this way: *"For He made Him who knew no sin to be sin for us, that we might become the righteousness of God in Him."* (2 Corinthians 5:21) And for people who have truly experienced grace, sin will have no dominion over them. Such people do not think of going around and killing others. God's grace causes them to not want to sin. They love God and don't want to do that. God's grace transforms them inwardly and permanently.

So don't ever call grace "cheap". It is not cheap! It may be free for you, but it is not cheap. It cost God His Son. It cost God the precious blood of His beloved Son. Grace is free for us today because Jesus paid the price for us to have it. It is now possible for us to experience undeserved favour, but only because of Jesus. That's why when you experience His grace, you fall in love with Him and out of love with sin!

Grace Is A Person

chapter 3

Grace Is A Person

Jesus Is The Reason For Our Blessing

D o you realise that Benjamin, his brothers and their father Jacob were all blessed because of Joseph? The slave who became the saviour of the world fed the world in a time of famine.

Through His Holy Spirit, God is opening our eyes to see that in these last days, the Benjamin Generation will be blessed because of

Jesus. You see, Jesus is our heavenly Joseph. Like Joseph, this undeserved favour that God has for us comes only because of Jesus. He took our place of condemnation and we take His place of blessing. He is the reason why God is gracious to us.

Grace Came By Jesus

In fact, Jesus is not just the reason why God showers His grace on us. Jesus **is** grace. Grace is not a doctrine. Grace is a person. Grace is Jesus Christ.

Let me explain. The Apostle John said,

> *"For the law was given through Moses, but grace and truth came through Jesus Christ."* (John 1:17)

Why go only for the gift? Why not go for the giver?

Notice that the law was **given**. That is impersonal. Grace **came**. Grace is personal and came in the person of Jesus.

When you have Jesus in your life, you have grace in your life and you have God's unmerited favour. This favour is unearned and undeserved. And when you have Him living on the inside of you, you have the power for true holiness living inside you. You have the power to prosper living inside you. You have the wisdom of God living inside you. When you have Jesus, you have everything.

Some Christians go to Jesus just for the blessings. Then, they go their own merry way and when the provisions run out, they run back to Him. Do you know that when such people come back, Jesus will still feed them? That is how good He is. He says that those who come to Him, He will in no wise cast out. (John 6:37)

But it doesn't have to be like that. Why go to Jesus only for the gift? Why not go for the giver? When you have Him, you have everything. I don't just want His hand of blessing, I want Him. I want Him every day. I want my heart to be full of Him.

Jesus Is Our Heavenly Joseph

If you are wondering why I am comparing Joseph to Jesus, why I am calling Jesus our heavenly

Joseph, it is because Joseph is a type of Jesus. When I use the word "type", I mean a picture or a symbol. So Joseph in the Old Testament is a picture of what our Saviour Jesus is like. Joseph symbolises Jesus. How? For a start, Joseph tended flocks. So did our Lord Jesus — He is the Good Shepherd.

Joseph's brothers hated and rejected him. Likewise, Jesus came to His own brothers in the flesh, the Jews, and they too rejected Him. John said that He came to His own, but His own did not receive Him. (John 1:11). Israel rejected Him. That is why they are in darkness. That is why they have been suffering since. The devil could attack them through the Holocaust because they rejected the covering of their Saviour.

But we must be careful when we talk about this. We must not become anti-Semitic. Some people think that the Jews killed Jesus. On the contrary, it was all of our sins that put Him on the cross. Jesus was not murdered. He laid down His life willingly. (John 10:17–18) And He did it because of our sins.

So don't blame the Jewish people. God has not rejected them and replaced them with the church. He loves the church. But He also loves the Jewish people. We are both seeds of Abraham. (Hebrews 11:12) The Jews are the natural seed, we are the spiritual seed. They are the sand on the seashore, we are the stars in heaven.

Another similarity between Joseph and Jesus is that Joseph's brothers did not recognise him the first time round. He was only recognised at his second appearance. It will be the same for Jesus. And during His second coming, all Israel will be saved.

Another parallel between Joseph and Jesus can be seen in how they both ministered to two criminals. In the dungeon, two prisoners came to Joseph for help. One lived, the other died. During the crucifixion, Jesus also had two criminals beside Him. One received eternal life, the other did not.

And by the way, of all his sons, whom did Jacob love the most? Joseph, of course! Likewise, God loves His Son the most.

As we have seen, Joseph was given the name Zaphnath-Paaneah, which means "saviour of the world". Jesus is the true Saviour. Joseph was raised to save the people from famine. He was able to feed Egypt, which is a picture of the Gentiles. Jesus is the bread of life. (John 6:35) Today, He feeds His church, which is predominantly Gentile. He is our spiritual as well as our physical sustenance.

You don't have to worry about an economic famine when you have the heavenly Joseph in your life. I don't care how bad the world's economy gets. When the famine was severe, Joseph had enough food for Egypt as well as for his brothers. Jesus has enough sustenance for all of us. We simply have to go to Him. He wants to pour His unmerited favour and blessings on us. Our heavenly Joseph wants to bless us, the Benjamin Generation.

Our Heavenly Joseph Loves Benjamin

Have you ever noticed that Joseph loved Benjamin the most? You will find that the first time Joseph wept when he saw his brothers was when Benjamin appeared. (Genesis 43:30)

Why is that? Because though all the brothers shared the same father, they didn't have the same mother. Only Joseph and Benjamin had the same father and mother. That means that though all Christians share the same Father, they don't all share the same mother.

Let me explain that. We all know who our Father is, right? God, of course. So who are the mothers? They are Rachel and Leah. And what do the two mothers represent? Rachel represents grace, while Leah represents the law.

There are some Christians who believe that we are still under the Ten Commandments. These Christians have Leah as their mother. But we, the Benjamin Generation, believe that God found fault with the old covenant, found fault with the law and He has established the new covenant of grace. Therefore, we have Rachel as our mother.

Unfortunately, some of those Christians who don't share the same mother as us, the Benjamin Generation, will persecute us. Remember that Ishmael, who was born of human performance, persecuted Isaac, who was born of promise. It is the same today. Those who insist on being under the law will persecute those who are under grace.

These same people accuse us of always preaching grace. They ask, "Why do you always talk about grace, grace, grace? Don't you know that God demands obedience?" They say that God demands that we obey the law. They accuse us of preaching "cheap grace". They think that if you don't give people the law, they will go out and do crazy things. They say that when we preach grace, we are giving people licence to sin.

> Because Jesus gave us the gift of no condemnation, we have the power to go and sin no more.

Let me say this again: When people experience God's grace, sin will have no dominion over them. Just look at what happened to the woman who was caught in adultery and brought to Jesus by the Pharisees. What did Jesus tell that woman? Most people will say, "He told her to go and sin no more." He did, but what did He say before that? He said, *"Neither do I condemn you."* (John 8:11)

Before we have the power to go and sin no more, we need to know that He does not condemn us. Because Jesus gave this woman the gift of no condemnation, she had the power to go and sin no more.

Isn't that beautiful? When we experience Jesus, we experience His grace that brings supernatural transformation. It is us, the Benjamin Generation, the ones who share the same Father and mother as Joseph, a type of Christ, who will experience His goodness that leads us to repentance. It is the Benjamin Generation who will experience this supernatural and lasting transformation.

Worshipping Our Heavenly Joseph

When we experience His goodness, our natural response is to worship Him. When we realise that Jesus is the reason for our blessing, our natural response should be to tell the Father all about Jesus' goodness.

When Joseph revealed his true identity to his brothers and told them about God's plan to bless them, he could not wait for them to tell his father Jacob about it. His command to them was, *"... tell my father of all my glory in Egypt, and of all that you have seen; and you shall hurry and bring my father down here."* (Genesis 45:13)

True worship is telling the Father of Jesus' glory. Whatever we hear preached to us, whatever we have seen in the Word, Jesus wants us to bring it back to the Father and say, "Oh, Father, the Lord Jesus is so beautiful! He is so full of grace, so full of mercy, so full of tender loving-kindness. How can I not love Him!"

> True worship does not flow out of emotions, but redemption.

When we talk like that, it is true worship. Worship is bringing Jesus to the Father. He is our burnt offering, our meal offering, our peace offering, our sin offering and our trespass offering. His work on the cross is so beautiful that it takes five offerings to represent what He did. And when you bring Jesus to the Father, when you extol His finished work on the cross, the Father is pleased. And He accepts you.

Don't misunderstand me. We are not accepted by what we **do**. We are blessed and accepted only because of what Jesus has **done**. True worship points back to what He has done.

The Benjamin Generation will be a generation that offers true worship — worship that exalts Jesus' finished work. And true worship does not flow out of emotions, but out of redemption.

Get Ready For The End-Time Blessings!

chapter 4

Get Ready For The End-Time Blessings!

Get Ready To Receive

I know that God wants to unleash His blessings on us in these end times. I know this because God is releasing this truth about the Benjamin Generation. So get ready to receive! When the 10 brothers first met Joseph in Egypt, they were imprisoned. But the moment Benjamin came to Egypt, there was no more jail-house talk. Grace was released and blessings followed!

Instead of prison food, they were welcomed into the palace for a feast. Their brother Joseph threw the feast for them. He had earlier declared that unless Benjamin came into his presence, he would not entertain them and there would be no bread. (Genesis 43:3–5) So when the brothers brought his youngest brother to him, Joseph's first instruction was "serve the bread". (Genesis 43:31)

Today, our heavenly Joseph is giving instructions to serve the bread. So Benjamin Generation, get ready for His end-time blessings! It's time for the feast!

Blessings For Israel

These end-time blessings are not just for the church, they are also for the Jewish people. God has so much blessing, He is pouring it out on both the seeds of Abraham — the natural seed and the spiritual seed.

Joseph didn't just bless Benjamin, he also blessed his 10 brothers. He gave instructions for the sacks of his 10 brothers to be filled with grain as well as the money which they had paid for the grain. These 10 brothers represent the Jewish people. Most Jews are still living under the old covenant, under the Ten Commandments. Yet, they are still blessed.

When Joseph's brothers returned for more grain, they told the steward, *"We do not know who put our money in our sacks."* (Genesis 43:22) Although the Jews are blessed, many of them don't know who is blessing them. They are a minority race, yet their achievements are beyond that of any other race. They have Nobel prize winners, key players in the movie industry, financial giants... the list is extensive and impressive.

> Tithing will affect your future generations.

That is why Hitler opposed them. He was jealous because no matter where the Jews went, they would end up becoming rich. The natural seed of Abraham always seems to end up with money. And yet they don't know who put the money in their sacks. But we know who is blessing them. It is Jesus, the heavenly Joseph. He is blessing them because of their father Abraham.

Now, Abraham was a tither. He gave a tenth of all he had to Melchizedek, who was the pre-incarnate appearance of Jesus. This act affected his future generations. Paul said, *"Even Levi, who receives tithes, paid tithes through Abraham, so to speak, for he was still in the loins of his father when Melchizedek met him."* (Hebrews 7:9–10) When I read this, I wondered how this was possible. Levi was the great-grandson of Abraham. He was one of Benjamin's brothers, so how could he have paid tithes through Abraham?

Then, the Lord told me, "Son, tithing will affect your future generations." When Abraham tithed, God counted it as if his great-grandson Levi had tithed as well. And for that, Levi was blessed. Can you imagine, when I tithe, my little daughter Jessica gets blessed too!

Folks, please understand that this does not mean that you can buy the blessings of God. You cannot buy God's blessings. You cannot bribe Him. God blesses you freely because He chooses to. When you tithe, when you give Him a tenth of what you have, you are just honouring Him. And when you honour Him, you are blessed. And more than that, when you tithe, God treats it as if your future generations have tithed. And He blesses them as well!

Sadly, although the Jewish people are financially blessed by God, Israel as a nation has rejected their Saviour. God showed a picture of this rejection in the binding of Simeon. When Joseph told his brothers to bring Benjamin to Egypt, he bound Simeon and kept him imprisoned until Benjamin returned.

Of all the brothers, why did Joseph pick Simeon? It was strategic, it was a prophetic act. You see, Simeon means "hearing". By that act, Joseph was prophesying that the hearing of the Jewish people would be bound for a while. And when Jesus was born, God wanted to release hearing to His people. An old man by the name of Simeon came to the temple and prophesied over the baby Jesus. (Luke 2:25–35) But the Jewish people still refused to heed the prophecy pointing to Jesus as their Messiah. Even today, when you talk about Jesus, most of the Jewish people refuse to hear.

But do you know what? God's heart is tender towards His people. When Joseph revealed his identity to his brothers, fear gripped them. And so he spoke to them with tenderness:

> Genesis 45:5,7–8
>
> [5]But now, do not therefore be grieved or angry with yourselves because you sold me here; for God sent me before you to preserve life... [7]And God sent me before you to preserve a posterity for you in the earth, and to save your lives by a great deliverance. [8]So now it was not you who sent me here, but God; and He has made me a father to Pharaoh, and lord of all his house, and a ruler throughout all the land of Egypt.

Our heavenly Joseph will not condemn His people. Although they have rejected Him, He responds to them with tenderness.

Blessings For The Church

If God blesses the natural seed of Abraham, even though they have rejected Him, how much more will He bless the church! The devil has tried to keep the church poor for a long time. He wants us to believe that holiness means having holes in our shoes! And he has succeeded for a period of time. That's why we have the saying "as poor as a church mouse". But no more! God wants the end-time church to be prosperous.

He wants the Benjamin Generation to experience both spiritual and financial blessings. Let me ask you this: If you see a five-dollar note and a hundred-dollar note on the floor, which one would you pick up? I once asked someone this and he looked at me uncertainly. I said, "You would pick up both, right?" "Yyyyesss!" he stammered. He was afraid to say "Yes" because he was an honest man and he wouldn't want to take someone else's money.

Of course, if you see money on the floor and it belongs to someone else, please return it to the person. I only use this illustration to prove a point. And the point is that some Christians are wasting time arguing about whether God wants to bless us spiritually or materially. Well, the answer is both! Take all the spiritual blessings and on top of that, God wants to give us material blessings as well. Who do you think placed all the sapphires, diamonds, rubies and other precious minerals in the earth? The devil? No, the devil cannot create a single thing! He can only pervert what God has created. It is your heavenly Father who is the creator of all these good things.

Joseph also gave his brothers clothing. Now, men, don't be afraid to say it: "Wow! Clothing! Armani suits! Silk ties!" Joseph knew the value of quality clothes. His father had given him a coat of many colours when he was much younger. Now, here is something interesting — Benjamin received five times more than his brothers! He was also given 300 pieces of silver. And that was only for the journey home!

Joseph also sent back with them 10 donkeys **loaded** with the good things of Egypt. Let's be honest, folks, the good things of Egypt are not the good things of Canaan. The good things of Egypt are literally the good things of the world. They are not spiritual blessings, they are material possessions that the world desires. So God loads us even with these benefits. Now, I like that! That's the only type of "fit" I'd ever want — a bene**fit**!

Blessings — A Key To Spiritual Revival

You will find that when God blesses us, the world takes notice and begins to realise that Jesus is alive. This is what happened to Jacob.

> Genesis 45:26–28, KJV
> ²⁶And told him, saying, Joseph is yet alive, and he is governor over all the land of Egypt. And Jacob's heart fainted, for he believed them not. ²⁷And they told him all the words of Joseph, which he had said unto them: and when he saw the wagons which Joseph had sent to carry him, the spirit of Jacob their father revived: ²⁸And Israel said, It is enough; Joseph my son is yet alive: I will go and see him before I die.

When Jacob's sons told him that Joseph was alive, at first, he didn't believe them. It was only when he **saw** the wagons — the evidence of the blessings — that he believed. Like Jacob, the world needs to **see** God's goodness in and through us. The evidence of God's blessings in our lives helps them believe in a good God.

And the Bible says that Jacob's spirit was revived. There is a lesson here. How do you have a spiritual revival? By letting the world **see** God's blessings in your life.

Some of you will say, "Pastor Prince, this is not talking of a spiritual revival." But the Bible says Jacob's **spirit** was revived when he saw the wagons. Look at what happened to Jacob after his spirit was revived. The Holy Spirit changed his name to Israel.

Material blessings are an important key to spiritual revival.

The name Jacob means "supplanter" or "deceiver". He received this name because during his birth, he held on to his brother's heel and he tried to overtake his older twin. (Genesis 25:26) Later, he ended up cheating his brother Esau of his birthright and blessing. (Genesis 27:36)

But after Jacob had an encounter with God, he was given the name Israel, which means "prince with God". (Genesis 32:28) Then, in Genesis 45, after Jacob's spirit was revived, the Holy Spirit purposely used the name Israel. Why would God suddenly start calling him Israel? The reason is that God wanted to show us that Jacob had become a believer again. He **saw** the wagons — the evidence of the blessings — and he believed. This tells me that material blessings are an important key to spiritual revival.

God Blessed Me With A BMW

When Jacob saw the wagons, his spirit was revived. Now, let's relate this to the 21st century. What is a modern-day wagon? It's a car, of course. Can you believe it? God wants to give us wagons!

I first received this revelation from God one day when I went to buy a car. At the time, I didn't have the money to buy the car that I finally bought. I wanted to buy a BMW, but I only had enough money for a 3 Series or 5 Series, not for a 7 Series.

But because it was a time of recession, car prices had dropped drastically. On top of that, the Government was giving a special rebate. In the end, it worked out that with the money I had, I could actually buy a 7 Series BMW.

One of my pastors went with me to view the car. He looked at it and told me to buy the car. He called it "a very good buy". So I bought it and I remember the manager remarked to me that I was very smart to buy it. Now, do you think I am smart? I must admit to you that I don't know much about cars. I have no idea about the market value of cars. But two months later, the price of my car shot right up. In fact, if I had sold it then, I would have made more than $30,000! Now, that was the blessing of God!

Actually, I got cold feet when I thought of driving a 7 Series BMW. At that time, no pastor in Singapore was driving such a car. I looked at that car. It was so beautiful and yet, I began to imagine myself driving it and hearing people say, "Oh, that pastor must have taken money from the church to buy that car!" But I didn't and I don't now. I **never** take an offering for my personal needs.

I went home and prayed, "Lord, people are going to talk. Please show me if this miracle is from you." I was concerned about my testimony because as a pastor, I have a responsibility to the people. I didn't want my actions to affect people's attitude towards God or to damage their personal relationship with God. I knew the Lord could bless me with this car, but I didn't want my decision to cause people to stumble in their faith. I wanted to honour the Lord.

That was when God showed me how the Holy Spirit used the name Israel **after** Jacob saw the wagons. He made me realise that many times, people find it hard to believe mere words. Words are often not enough. They need to first **see** and then they will say, "God **is** good."

Let me tell you that God really has a sense of humour. After He showed me the scripture about Jacob seeing the wagons, He told me what BMW means — "Behold, My Wagon"!

I knew that when I started driving the car, there would be a few people who would criticise me. But I went ahead and bought the car for the sake of the many. I wanted to let them see that God is good. I wanted them to know that He can give His servant a dream car. And I didn't even start out with enough money! I didn't have to take up an offering for it. God simply provided.

My family and I enjoy the car, but I know it's just a car. I'm more captured by the love of

God for me. He gave me a dream car! He really loves me!

Awed By His Grace

Sometimes, when God shows His people grace, they cannot believe it. Sometimes, they even reject it. They say "No!" to His blessings. Singaporeans understand this attitude. We don't believe in a free lunch. We think a free gift with no strings attached is just not possible. It's strange, but people find it hard to receive grace. They are not comfortable receiving anything for free. They think that there must be a catch.

> You don't need the Holy Spirit to understand the law. But you do need the Holy Spirit to understand grace.

Joseph's brothers were very fearful when they found that the money they had paid for the grain was returned to their sacks. (Genesis

42:27–28) Grace is not normal. It's not natural. In fact, it's supernatural!

People understand law, but they don't understand grace. If you were to walk down Orchard Road in Singapore's main shopping belt and ask people, "How do you get to heaven?" they will tell you, "Do good... Don't do evil... Don't kill... Don't steal... " They will basically tell you to obey the Ten Commandments.

No one would tell you, "We go to heaven by grace." That proves that the law is natural to people. Grace is not natural. You don't need the Holy Spirit to understand the law. But you do need the Holy Spirit to understand grace. You need the Holy Spirit to understand that it is by grace, not by the law, that we are saved. It takes the Holy Spirit to reveal to us that Jesus took our beating so that today, we can have His blessings.

Benjamin did nothing to deserve any of the blessings. He just received. And just because Joseph loved him, he received five times more than any of his brothers.

Prosperity With A Purpose

Do you realise that Joseph instructed his servants to pack his brothers' sacks with grain, but in Benjamin's sack, the servants were also told to plant a silver cup? The sacks represent financial blessing. What Joseph did for Benjamin, our heavenly Joseph wants to do for us in these last days. He wants to prosper His people.

But look at what happened to Benjamin. Joseph instructed the servants to plant a silver cup in Benjamin's sack. That silver cup represents redemption. In Luke 22:42, Jesus prayed, *"Father, if it is Your will, take this cup away from Me; nevertheless not My will, but Yours, be done."* The depiction of silver to represent redemption is very consistent in the Bible. In the Old Testament, people used silver to pay the redemption price. Look at Leviticus 5:15:

> [15]"If a person commits a trespass, and sins unintentionally in regard to the holy things of the Lord, then he shall bring to the Lord as his trespass offering a ram without blemish from the flocks, with your valuation

in shekels of silver according to the shekel
of the sanctuary, as a trespass offering.

The silver cup which represents redemption
was planted in Benjamin's sack. Today, that
silver cup represents the sum total of all our
sins. And do you know why the cup is empty?
Because Jesus drank every drop of the filth of our
sins so that today, we can experience the fullness
of His blessings! The
cup is empty so we can
receive the fullness of
His blessings!

> We have
> prosperity with
> a purpose, and
> the purpose is to
> reveal Jesus to a
> lost and dying
> world.

Isn't it amazing
that God didn't plant
the silver cup of
redemption in the sacks
of the other brothers,
only in Benjamin's?
He is blessing us, the
Benjamin Generation, to be a blessing and to
proclaim Jesus' finished work at the cross.

Now, here is another amazing truth: The
grain in the sack was wheat, which is used to
make bread. Now, bread also represents the

Word of God. So this means that the sack not only represents prosperity, it also represents the Word of God. Which means that every time we, the Benjamin Generation, peek into the sack (in other words, every time we read the Word), what we see in the sack (the Word) is the silver cup (Jesus' redemption, the finished work of Jesus on the cross). Every time we read the Word, we see His redemption! We no longer see His judgment, we see the amazing grace of God! And that is what we will proclaim — His finished, complete and perfect work on the cross for us.

Jesus our heavenly Joseph loves us. And He wants to give the Benjamin Generation five times more blessings than any other generation. We are being given prosperity with a purpose, and the purpose is to reveal Jesus to a lost and dying world.

Don't let anyone preach the blessings of God out of your life. Don't let anyone rob you of the sense of grace that you have. All that you have is based on the finished work of Jesus.

Right now, God is raising up the Benjamin Generation. We are the last generation. And during these end times, there will be a famine.

But fear not, for He will provide the good things of Egypt. He will load us with food, wagons and clothing, and we will receive five times more. But we must always remember this: We receive it not because we deserve it, but because Jesus paid for it!

Salvation Prayer

If you would like to receive all that Jesus has done for you and make Him your Lord and Saviour, please pray this prayer:

Lord Jesus, thank You for loving me and dying for me on the cross. Your precious blood washes me clean of every sin. You are my Lord and my Savior, now and forever. I believe that You rose from the dead and that You are alive today. Because of Your finished work, I am now a beloved child of God and heaven is my home. Thank You for giving me eternal life, and filling my heart with Your peace and joy. Amen.

We Would Like To Hear From You

If you have prayed the salvation prayer, or if you have a testimony to share after reading this book, please send us an email at info@josephprince.com

Other Materials By Joseph Prince

We trust that you have been blessed reading this book. For more books and other resources such as message CDs and DVDs by Joseph Prince, or for more information, please visit our website at www.josephprince.com